WHAT YOU SHOULD KNOW ABOUT THE MASS

Charlene Altemose, MSC

Liguori
ONE LIGUORI DRIVE
LIGUORI MO 63057-9999
314.464.2500

Imprimi Potest:
James Shea, C.SS.R.
Provincial, St. Louis Province
The Redemptorists

Imprimatur:
Monsignor Maurice F. Byrne
Vice Chancellor, Archdiocese of St. Louis

ISBN 0-89243-462-7
Library of Congress Catalog Card Number: 92-72595

Copyright © 1992, Liguori Publications
Printed in the United States of America
98 99 00 01   8 7 6 5

All rights reserved. No part of this booklet may be reproduced, stored in a retrieval system, or transmitted without the written permission of Liguori Publications.

Scripture quotations are taken from the *The New American Bible with Revised New Testament and the Revised Psalms*, copyright © 1991, by the Confraternity of Christian Doctrine, Washington, D.C., and are used with permission. All rights reserved.

Excerpts from the English translation of *The Roman Missal*, copyright © 1973, International Committee on English in the Liturgy, Inc. (ICEL), are used with permission. All rights reserved.

Cover design by Chris Sharp
Interior art by Andy Willman

CONTENTS

Introduction 5
Chapter 1: The Mass — Yesterday and Today 9
Chapter 2: Sacrifice, Thanksgiving, and Praise 15
Chapter 3: Persons Involved in Liturgy 22
Chapter 4: Where Liturgy Is Celebrated 27
Chapter 5: Church and Liturgical Furnishings 30
Chapter 6: The Primary Liturgical Symbols 35
Chapter 7: The Liturgical Year and Feast Days 40
Chapter 8: Structure and Parts of the Mass 46
Conclusion 64

INTRODUCTION

Catholics agree that the Mass is central to the practice of faith. But ask what the Mass means or how important it is and you get a variety of replies.

In preparation for this booklet, I experimented with my assumptions. I chose a fairly large parish, one with six Masses each weekend and a full parking lot during each Mass.

Unassumingly, I roamed the parking lot and randomly chose my "victims." I asked, "Why are you at Mass today? What does it mean for you?" The responses were varied.

"Well, it's the thing for me to do on Sundays. I was raised Catholic, and I've always gone to Mass on Sunday."

"Because the Church says so."

"I come to ask God for help for the week ahead."

"I'm not too much of a churchgoer but now my boy's sick and I really need God."

"I came with a friend who happens to be Catholic, so I thought this is as good as going to any other church."

"I'm a college student and have to write a term paper on what Catholics believe."

Rarely did someone respond, "I come to give honor and praise to God…to join with my fellow believers in worship."

The results of that survey confirmed my conviction of the need for a booklet such as this.

Those who attend Mass on Sunday are faith-filled people, yet their faith may not be properly focused. It isn't disrespect; it's a lack of awareness and a poor formation of faith. It reminds me of those Jesus spoke of when he said, "This people honors me with their lips, but their hearts are far from me" (Matthew 15:8).

Imagine a person who knows nothing about football going to the Super Bowl just to eat the hot dogs sold at the stadium concession stands. Focusing narrowly on the hot dogs, this person misses the human passion, the excitement of the fans, and the athletic drama of the game itself.

I don't intend to compare the Mass to the Super Bowl. But this example demonstrates how we can overlook the rich realities of something simply because we lack understanding and a proper focus. In this booklet, I hope to provide insights and reflections on what the Mass is and can be.

The believing community gathering for liturgy can be an exciting faith experience. It can transform, heal, and empower us on our personal spiritual journey. When we expand our awareness of what great gift the Eucharist is, we participate more fully in the experience. When we get caught up in the celebration, the Mass is a credible, visible sign of Jesus' continuing presence.

This booklet also serves as a formation tool, explaining how and why the Mass has changed in recent decades. To appreciate the new rites, we need to become "re-formed" worshipers. We need to understand what liturgical worship is all about.

Primarily, this booklet provides insights for Catholics who regularly attend Mass. Many others, however, can benefit: those who come "just because" will become more purposeful. Those who think of Mass as an obligation will learn to appreciate it as a great privilege and gift. Catholics who nostalgically remember Mass the "way it used to be" will better understand the new liturgy as it is celebrated today. Those who hanker for the Latin language, the Gregorian chant, and quiet time for their own prayers will better understand the rationale behind all the changes.

This booklet is for those who wish to make their worship truly meaningful. Those who want to know why we do what we do at Mass will find many useful insights.

Those who are searching for a meaningful way to serve the Lord, those who are curious about what goes on behind Catholic church doors, and those who just never took the time to delve into what the Eucharist is about: all will find in these pages some valuable material for reflection.

Priests and preachers, too, can benefit from this work. It presents explanations, information, and insights at the layperson's level. Priests and preachers can learn straightforward, nontechnical ways to explain beliefs and practices to the average Catholic.

I use both a devotional and practical approach rather than a theoretical or theological approach. Although some aspects of the liturgy will be explained in depth, I hope to provide a prayerful way to make Eucharist a significant faith experience — not just something we do as Catholics. My approach presents the who, where, what, when, how, and why of our liturgical celebration. This booklet also contains many practical guidelines on attitudes the worshiper can cultivate to make liturgy meaningful.

In *The Inward Journey* (Liguori Publications, 1991), Marilyn Norquist Gustin calls the Mass "a microcosm of our spiritual life which can re-center us each time we participate." This booklet elaborates and expands on that basic practical theme.

Chapter 1

THE MASS – YESTERDAY AND TODAY

All families have experienced the death of a loved one. After the funeral, family members often gather at the old homestead. They reminisce, relate stories, and gather mementos of the loved one. They share experiences of how the person touched their lives. By way of these simple rituals, the family keeps alive the memory of one who is no longer with them.

That's what Jesus' friends and disciples did after he was no longer with them. The small group of disciples came together and recalled the times they spent with Jesus. They shared their experiences and feelings of how Jesus affected their lives. They came together on Sunday to commemorate Jesus' rising from the dead. Their Jewish day of rest, the Sabbath, was observed the previous day in the synagogue.

As time went on, this small band of people came to realize that Jesus was the Messiah, the Promised One. They read the words of the prophets that foretold of the Messiah. They read the letters Paul wrote to the various communities of faith. Later, they shared the written accounts that were to become the gospels.

They divided their food and belongings with others. They shared bread and wine in the same way they did as practicing Jews. They remembered Jesus and shared the bread and wine as Jesus' body and blood. They kept alive the memory of Christ.

These informal gatherings became the chief way that the early Christians worshiped God and carried on the spirit and mission of Christ. Sunday replaced the Sabbath as their weekly holy day. As the Church expanded and grew, the Mass evolved from a simple community gathering to ritualized formal worship.

In 1962, Pope John XXIII convened the Second Vatican Council. The purpose of the Council was to recapture the simplicity and spirit of the early Church and to make the Church more meaningful for our present age. Because the Mass is the center of Catholic worship, liturgical reform was one of the first innovations the Vatican Council undertook. The Second Vatican Council introduced changes and options in our worship to promote greater understanding and laity participation.

Today, the Mass is strikingly different from the way it was before the liturgical changes. The altar, the focal point of worship, has been turned around; the priest faces the people. The language of the people has replaced Latin. The laity serve as ministers in various liturgical capacities. The congregation participates with responses and singing.

Although the presider and the assisting ministers set the tone, all who take part are responsible for making worship meaningful. All these changes contribute toward making liturgy a rich faith experience for both the individual and the community.

Our coming together in worship is called "Mass" because we are sent out as a people and as a community in "mission" to spread the Good News. It's also referred to as "liturgy," from the Greek *leitourgia,* which means "work of the people"; as "Eucharist," which means "thanksgiving"; and as the "breaking of bread" or the "Lord's Supper," as we recall the sacred eve of Jesus' death. In this booklet, these terms are used interchangeably.

We Gather

The Mass is the primary way Catholics worship God. In the Mass, the Word becomes flesh. In a sense, our faith becomes flesh, too, as we act out what we believe.

A good analogy to the spirit of the Mass is the spirit of a reunion. How exhilarating it is when a group of people gather because they have something significant in common: family, school, or some historical experience. The camaraderie they experience brings to life an integral part of their common past. Their coming together binds them in closer unity and keeps alive the connectedness they share today as a result of their common history.

As Catholics, we share in the life and mission of Jesus in this same way. We express this belief as we come together in prayerful unity at Mass. Although we pray in a variety of ways, the community gathering at Mass is the soul of our Catholic worship. In this single act of worship, we keep alive the spirit of Jesus. If Jesus had lived, died, and rose from the dead and no one had noticed, his mission would have been in vain. But we did notice — and we do remember.

Grace and salvation flow from God through Jesus to us. We, the people of God, receive and embody this grace and salvation. Our faith enlivens and animates the Church.

The Mass essentially is a gathering of a community of people who share these common beliefs. The ordained priest presides at Mass and consecrates the bread and wine into the body and blood of Christ, laypersons serve in various roles as liturgical ministers, and the community joins in offering the Mass.

In celebrating the Mass, we are continuing to do what the first Christians did. We gather and witness to the belief that Christ lives on through our liturgical worship and faith-filled assembly. Through liturgy, we witness more vibrantly to what we really are: the people of God, the Body of Christ, the Church. The more vibrant the worshiping community, the more intense and visible will Christ's presence be manifest in the world.

We come together, celebrate our common belief, and worship the Lord in a public act of faith. When the gathering of the community of believers gives life to the liturgy, then the sacred action of the Mass is more clearly recognized as "God-with-us."

We Remember

In *How Green Was My Valley,* Richard Llewellyn wrote, "There's no fence around time that's gone. You can redeem time and have it again, if only you remember." Remembering is powerful. It reactivates and keeps a past reality alive. Memory energizes us; our past experiences go on and on. When we recapture a moment in time by remembering, we bring into our midst something we thought was gone.

The eucharistic celebration provides us a particular opportunity to remember God's goodness and blessings. We recall our own failings and our need for asking God's pardon. We remember how God intervened in human history. In the Hebrew Scriptures, we recall how the Israelites experienced and responded to God's revelation and how the prophets prepared them for the Day of the Lord. In the gospels, we remember Jesus' life. In the epistles and the Acts of the Apostles, we are reminded of the spread of the early Church.

Most especially, we remember that Jesus remains with us. At the Last Supper, he offered bread and wine to the Father "in remembrance" and gave this same gift to us as his body and blood. The entire Mass is the sacred memory and presence of Jesus living on throughout time in the Eucharist and in the hearts of believers.

We Celebrate

Celebrations are necessary for sane human living. They are a welcome break in the routine of the daily humdrum. Through a meaningful celebration, we capture the feeling and emotion of an event — and we become involved. Weddings, graduations, athletic events, birthday parties, and ordinary get-togethers are made special through celebrations. We celebrate with others, for there's no joy in celebrating alone. In unison with others, we capture the exhilarating mood and spirit of the occasion.

At Mass we celebrate — as one body — what we have come to believe about Jesus. At the Last Supper, Jesus identified himself with bread and wine, blessed and shared. Jesus' life and death is celebrated in a sacramental way through the consecration of the bread and wine into his sacred body and blood.

We actually relive and celebrate in sign and symbol who Jesus was, who he is, and who he will be. In the Eucharist, we celebrate all of time in a single act of worship. We proclaim in faith, "Christ has died, Christ is risen, Christ will come again."

We Ritualize

We celebrate: *we*. Liturgy is not like a symphony where we sit back and take it all in. We are not spectators at the celebration of the Mass. The Mass belongs to every one of us. We give the celebration its life. Without our deep and meaningful involvement, Christ's presence in our midst in the liturgy goes ignored.

In all of creation, only humans can give deeper meaning and significance to words, actions, or things. We plant trees, exchange rings, erect monuments, march for a cause, prepare special meals; we put into action what we feel and want to express. Only humans can ritualize. Because it is natural for us to reach beyond our own world to that which is Greater, the most mundane can become a sacred ritual when we assign sacred meaning to it. Ritual spells out what we celebrate; it enlarges and intensifies the ordinary and makes the ordinary more than ordinary.

At Mass, everyday gestures and signs take on a new significance because they are raised to the plateau of worship. The human actions we perform and the things we use become signs of the action of God. Jesus wished to remain with us, so he used the ordinary things of life. At Mass, ritual actions enable us to make a meaningful connection with the sacred mysteries we remember and commemorate. The rituals we observe, therefore, must be meaningful so the sacredness and deeper significance of what we celebrate will not lie dormant or be lost.

When we become "ritual literate," we see with new eyes and experience new feelings. Like those who discover new worlds through reading, we are able to worship the Lord with new hearts as we discover the profound significance in the ritual of the Mass.

Chapter 2

SACRIFICE, THANKSGIVING, AND PRAISE

At liturgy, we acknowledge our dependence on God; we celebrate God's saving deeds in our life. Worship is a "way of being" before God.

To benefit most fully, we bring to Mass our inner sentiments and attitudes. We offer God our best, praising and thanking God and getting caught up in the mystery of God's love and presence.

We Sacrifice

The word *sacrifice* implies doing something hard to gain a greater good, or giving up something for a higher purpose. In baseball, there's a sacrifice play: the batter bunts so a runner can gain a base. Children sacrifice their pennies for the needy in mission lands. Parents sacrifice their own preferences for their children's welfare.

The Mass is a sacrifice in the sense that Jesus gave up his earthly life to bring about our salvation. When we participate in the Mass, we share in Jesus' mission of salvation.

We expand our notion of the Mass as a sacrifice when we consider the Latin root of the word *sacrifice*:

sacer and *facere,* which mean "to make holy." The earthly resources of bread and wine are made holy and transformed into the body and blood of Christ. At Mass, we, too, are transformed if we open ourselves to the salvation the Lord offers through his perfect sacrifice on Calvary.

The sufferings, injustices, and hardships we face along life's way are made holy through Jesus' sacrifice. We are thus empowered to bear all of life with more equanimity. Each eucharistic celebration is a means to overcome that which hinders our union with God.

We Give Thanks and Praise

When we praise and thank someone, we reach beyond ourselves, out to another. We die to self and consider the good of another. Through praise and appreciation, we acknowledge and affirm another.

Thanking and praising are not limited to human exchanges; in gratitude and with praise, we communicate with God as well. Of course, God does not need our praise; we praise God first for our own good. And although the Lord is satisfied with a simple "thank you," our liturgy ritualizes the kind of praise due the creator of the universe. The very word *eucharist* comes from the Greek word *eucharistia,* which means "to give thanks." The Mass expresses praise and thanks to God again and again: "We give you thanks"; "Thanks be to God."

Since all that we have and all that we are have come as gifts from the Lord, "it is right to give him thanks and praise" is our response at the opening of the eucharistic prayer. Throughout the Mass, the priest's prayers and our responses express thanks and praise.

We most perfectly praise God at Mass because every prayer is offered through Christ, our Lord.

When we respond "Amen," we are saying "Yes, Lord, I praise you, but my praise is limited and imperfect. Yet, when I join my praise and thanksgiving with others at liturgy and offer my prayers through Jesus, my praise becomes most pleasing in your sight."

We Are Nourished and Healed

When I was growing up, mealtime was important. We ate together and shared all the happenings of our day. In this sharing, I felt the support and love of our family.

Today, a meal still has the impact of togetherness. When family and friends get together, when business associates wish to discuss matters, when celebrations are held, it usually involves food and/or drink.

Jesus knew the importance of a shared meal. When he asked us to remember him, he did so within the context of a special meal: the Jewish Passover. Our renewed liturgy portrays the Mass as a sacred meal.

The altar, simple and unadorned, is the table of the Lord. The universal food staples of bread and wine become the body and blood of Christ, our spiritual food and drink. As an intense sign of our unity, we share the sacred meal at the table of the Lord with others of our faith community.

In the same way, when the priest changes bread and wine into the body and blood of Christ, we, too, are changed. We respond to God's grace in the celebration of the liturgy and in receiving the precious body and blood of our Lord; we are transformed into the likeness of Jesus. Nutritionists say that we are what we eat. Jesus promises more: "I am the living bread that came down from heaven; whoever eats this bread will live forever; and the bread that I will give is my flesh for the life of the world" (John 6:51).

A dimension of the nourishment characteristic of the Eucharist is "gift." Gifts are special ways that we say "You are special to me." Whenever we wish to express someone's specialness or recall some occasion, we give a gift. It's not the value of the gift but the thought that counts. A true gift is one given without strings attached; it is given unconditionally. When we open our hearts, others are open to us and reciprocate.

At Mass, we gift the Lord with our presence. We gift the Lord with our love. We gift the Lord through our worshiping together. We gift the Lord at liturgy in many ways. It's the perfect way to say, "Jesus, you mean so much to me and I am grateful."

In return, God gifts us with his Son, Jesus, in the Eucharist. God loves each of us, cares about us, and knows all our concerns. When I was a child, it was so hard for me to understand this, since there are so many people in the world. How could God care specifically about *me?* I'm so small and not very important.

This was answered for me on a poster I received. It shows a small child in the midst of a field of dandelions, holding one of the little blooms, and looking at it in sheer delight, oblivious to the thousands of other dandelions. The caption reads: "God loves each of us as if there were one of us."

Isaiah wrote: "I have called you by name: you are mine" (Isaiah 43:1). Let us remember this as we approach our God in worship. Our God looks at each of us lovingly and asks, "What can I do for you today?" Gift the Lord with your love.

Forgiveness is also a part of this experience. We all know the comfort we find in the words "I'm sorry" and "You're forgiven." Forgiveness is a healing balm.

Each Mass is a new beginning; we are given the

opportunity to express our sorrow for our past shortcomings and to experience God's healing forgiveness.

The change of the bread and wine into the body and blood of Christ enables us, too, to be transformed, to be made holy.

During Mass, we pray: "We thank you for counting us worthy to stand in your presence and serve you."

We pray for forgiveness: "Forgive us our trespasses." We beg for cleansing and renewal: "May this holy offering cleanse and renew us." We hope for healing: "Lord, I am not worthy to receive you, but only say the word and I shall be healed."

Of course, we're never completely healed. At Mass, however, we come before the Lord in all our weakness, in all our sinfulness, and we open ourselves to divine healing. God responds in love.

We are reminded of the extent of this love as we look up at the cross which is before us at Mass. The cross is the supreme sign of healing and forgiveness. Our eucharistic celebration taps the infinite resources of love flowing from the cross.

We Are Faithful

It's a human need to want to understand everything around us. That's the way explorers and discoverers expand their horizons and grow in knowledge. Faithful to the unknown, they venture forward in a quest to understand. Similarly, to get in touch with God, we need to venture faithfully into the mystery of the eucharistic celebration.

The more we try to fathom its wonder, the more profound is it a mystery of faith. Faith, as a leap into the unknown, provides spiritual nourishment that we cannot perceive in the present moment. Like eating a balanced diet: we cannot directly perceive the effects, but we realize it's for our good.

At Mass, we come face to face with a divine mystery we cannot fully understand, but we choose to be faithful to that mystery. In an act of faith, we open our hearts to the treasures that "eye has not seen, and ear has not heard" (1 Corinthians 2:9). We approach the liturgy in a spirit of readiness, allowing the Lord to work in our hearts.

The Lord sees our full humanity: what we are and what we can be.

Often these two elements are worlds apart in our being. The aim of our life is to meld these two realities into an integrated whole.

Our faithfulness to the mystery of the liturgy provides opportunities for us to live up to this spiritual potential.

We Are One Body

The Mass is sacrifice, thanksgiving, praise, nourishment, healing, giving, and receiving. No one single aspect of the Mass encompasses all of these. It's like a precious jewel: beautiful from every angle. We've seen that the Mass can be defined in so many different ways and called by many different names. The Mass means different things to different persons.

Yet, we come to the altar as a common and needy people. Although individually we may focus on our own need, the Mass satisfies all of us. No one goes away empty-handed. The Mass provides the spiritual grace and peace we each need to face life's situations with the eyes of God. At Mass, we get our spiritual lenses adjusted so we can see from God's vantage point.

As one body, we recognize our entire faith experience of the Lord in each eucharistic celebration.

The Mass encompasses all we believe about God's ineffable love for us.

As one body in a single act of worship, we give God our praise and thanks. It's the most perfect way we respond to Jesus' final invitation: "Do this in memory of me" (Luke 22:19).

As one body, we renew and deepen our commitment to our baptismal vows each time we celebrate Eucharist. At every Mass, we remember our common heritage, we celebrate our common faith, we ritualize our common bond as God's chosen people. To make Mass a once-a-year or special-occasion event is to diminish the communal dimension of the Body of Christ.

As one body, we meet our Lord whenever, wherever, and however Eucharist is celebrated. Whether Mass is celebrated in a grass hut in a distant mission country, in a cathedral with all pomp and circumstance, in an overcrowded parish church with babies screaming and people squashed together, or in the quiet of a sick room, the Mass is equally sacred and pleasing to the Lord. As one body, we are united with Christ in profound faith and mystery.

Chapter 3

PERSONS INVOLVED IN LITURGY

My favorite television programs are those that take me on a behind-the-scenes tour. Whether I'm watching the Olympics, the Super Bowl, the Space Shuttle, a White House event, or a circus, I enjoy the event more and understand it better when I'm given a glimpse of its inner workings. I marvel at the many details that must be meticulously observed and executed to ensure smooth operations.

Even a simple happening, the family meal for example, requires preparation and certain routines. The same is true about the Mass. Liturgy doesn't automatically happen; it is no instant miracle. Much work, dedication, and preparation are required to celebrate the Eucharist. Often these details are taken for granted. When we know what goes into preparing for the Mass, we can be more attentive and appreciative at the celebration.

In the next several chapters, we consider the persons, places, and things that give meaning and purpose to liturgy. We consider the who, where, what, and when of liturgy.

In the liturgy, we gather as a people of God in a

community celebration. There are many persons who contribute toward providing a fitting liturgy.

The sacrament of holy orders empowers bishops, priests, and deacons to carry out the sanctifying mission of the Church in a specific way.

Ordained Ministers

Bishops: As the ecclesiastical leaders of a diocese, bishops ordain priests and ordinarily confer the sacrament of confirmation. Bishops appoint priests to carry out specific roles in the diocese, to preside at worship, and to administer the sacraments. Deacons share in liturgical and pastoral services.

Priest: An ordained priest presides at the liturgy. He is either a diocesan priest directly responsible to the bishop or he belongs to a religious community, such as the Redemptorists, Jesuits, or Carmelites. During the Mass, the priest consecrates the sacred species and says the main prayers. More than one priest celebrating the liturgy is called concelebration, and the priests assisting the presider are called concelebrants.

Deacon: One of the most significant changes in the post-Vatican II Church is the restoration of the permanent diaconate. Although the diaconate has existed in the Church from its earliest days, the pre-Vatican II Church recognized only transitional deacons, those preparing for the priesthood. Today, this ministry enables married or single men to be ordained and to share more fully in the Church's ministry and liturgy.

An ordained deacon, whether transitional or permanent, assists the priest at Mass. He can acclaim the gospel, preach, give specific directives to the assembly, and distribute Communion.

The Community of Faith

The community of the faithful play no less significant role than the ordained ministers. The community prays along with the presiding priest. Because Mass is the community at worship, a priest cannot celebrate Mass without others present. There must be at least one person in attendance.

Lay Liturgical Ministers

Lay ministers become involved in the liturgy in response to a call to serve. Through this faith-response, they perform a role of service. The liturgical ministers aid the assembly to participate more meaningfully. By their demeanor and decorum, liturgical ministers convey a sense of the meaning of the sacred rituals.

Liturgical leader: A liturgical leader lends order and unity to the celebration. He or she gives specific directives to the assembly, especially on special occasions or solemn feasts.

Commentator: The commentator announces the theme, prays the general intercessions, and makes other announcements.

Acolyte or altar server: The altar server leads the processional, lights the candles, and assists the priest at the altar by holding the book and placing the vessels on the altar.

Lector: The lector, or reader, proclaims the Scripture. This ministry is truly a sacred trust, for in the lector's proclamation, the Word becomes flesh within the assembly. This noble task demands a deep faith combined with skill in oral communication.

Cantor: The cantor is the leader of song. He or she leads the assembly in song, sings certain solo parts, and rehearses new hymns with the assembly before Mass.

Presenters of the gifts: The gifts of bread and wine are brought to the priest by members of the assembly. These presenters are usually chosen beforehand. Oftentimes, persons will ask to carry the gifts; the day may be a special occasion for them or the Mass is being offered for a family member.

Eucharistic ministers: One of the more obvious innovations of Vatican II is the commissioning of laypersons to distribute Communion during Mass. It is a change that encourages the laity to participate more fully in their role as a priestly people. It's also a practical change because more people receive Communion and there are fewer priests. The eucharistic minister, like all the faithful, is called to exemplify in life what is said to each communicant: "The Body of Christ."

Music ministers: Music is a vital part of worship. In order to promote fitting liturgy, parishes need to give priority to music and utilize the giftedness of persons. The music team can include the music minister, choir director, choir, musicians, and cantor.

Ministers of hospitality: An air of friendliness and openness is necessary when we assemble for worship. People need to feel welcome. Some parishes have official greeters who welcome the worshipers and offer a kind word. This amenity is especially encouraging to visitors, those who are new to the area, or those attending Mass for the first time at a particular church.

Ushers perform a vital task of hospitality in helping persons find adequate seating. It's frustrating to walk into a crowded church and not be able to find a seat. The usher also passes the collection plate or basket at the appointed times.

Sacristan and sexton: The sacristan and the sexton do not enjoy high profiles, yet they are a vital part of the liturgical team. They work quietly and perform indispensable services behind-the-scenes.

The sacristan takes care of the nitty-gritty tasks: laundering linens and vestments; polishing the sacred vessels; decorating the altars; ordering the wine, hosts, and flowers; setting the altar for Mass; and many other tasks that need to be done.

The sexton is in charge of the overall upkeep of the church and its grounds. They are called "sextons" because in early days they summoned the peasants to prayer by ringing the church bells at the hour of "sext": noontime. Their tasks have changed with the changing times. Today, they ring the bells by flipping the "on" switch. As a security guard, heat-and-air-conditioner controller, gardener, lawn manicurist, mechanic, and electrician, the sexton is the parish's multifaceted expert.

Chapter 4

WHERE LITURGY IS CELEBRATED

Routinely, liturgy is celebrated in a church, a sacred place conducive to prayer and worship. The first impression one receives on entering should be a sense of reverence and sacred simplicity. The overall environment and decor remind us of the transcendent and aid us in praising God.

The Church has adopted creative art and architecture of human handiwork from every age and culture. Decorative styles vary according to contemporary customs, artistic preferences, or available resources.

Locations for Liturgy

Since the time of Constantine (A.D. 313), Christians have worshiped in places specifically built for liturgical celebrations. Though architectural designs have varied over the centuries, churches remain staunch symbols of the spiritual in the midst of the people. Today, churches stress noble simplicity, promote unity, and encourage participation of the worshiping community.

Basilica or shrine: A place of worship is designated as a basilica or shrine because of its antiquity, historical or architectural importance, or specific devotion. Basilicas and shrines often serve as places of pilgrimage. The best-known shrine in the United States is the National Shrine of the Immaculate Conception in Washington, D.C.

Cathedral: The main church of a diocese is the cathedral where the bishop conducts major diocesan ceremonies: ordinations and the blessing of the holy oils on Holy Thursday.

Parish church: The layperson has his or her most immediate contact and association with the Church through the local parish. It's in a parish church that one usually attends Mass.

A Catholic may attend Mass in any Catholic church. For the good of the faith community and the individual, it is best for a Catholic to identify with a specific parish usually determined by geographical boundaries. Parish membership gives one a distinct identity and sense of belonging. The parish church also provides social, educational, charitable, and other spiritual activities and opportunities.

Mission church: Communities of faith that celebrate liturgy regularly and have a specific place for meeting but who have no resident pastor or administrator are designated as mission parishes.

Chapel: Chapels are specific places in institutions, hospitals, colleges, military bases, and so forth, that are used for prayer and worship. Mass can be celebrated in a chapel used for services of other denominations or other purposes. Attendant spiritual directors, whether ordained or not, act as chaplains.

Other places for worship: Mass can be celebrated in places other than a church. Whether it is held in the open air, an auditorium, arena, or in your own living room, the ordinary decorum and sacredness of the Mass must be preserved.

The Liturgical Environment

From early times, churches were built on the style of a basilica, a rectangular structure with a rounded niche at one end. The body of the church, the nave, was for worshipers; liturgy was celebrated in the semicircular area. Today, a church's inner arrangement is designed to provide greater participation for the assembly.

Nave: The nave is one of the two main sections of the church. It is the gathering place of the assembly. It should provide all that is conducive to proper worship: ample visibility, proper acoustics, spaciousness, and the amenities of any public gathering place. This area may be furnished with fixed or movable pews, chairs, or benches, with or without kneelers.

Sanctuary: The sanctuary is the area of the church where most of the liturgical activity takes place. Distinct from the nave, the sanctuary is usually elevated.

Baptistery: In most churches, there is a place reserved for baptisms. It can be either a simple font, a specific space, or a separate room.

Chapter 5
CHURCH AND LITURGICAL FURNISHINGS

Symbols are sensible realities that point to the world of the unseen or transcendent. Through symbolism, we express a reality bigger than what we experience with our senses.

Since symbols express our relationship with God, our worship takes place in the language of symbolism. The environment we experience, the objects we use, the prayers we speak, the words we hear, the bread we taste, the postures and gestures we assume, the music we play, the incense we smell: all these things say more than meets the eye. The Mass is a meaningful experience in direct proportion to the degree we understand and value the symbolism that lies behind what we experience with our senses.

Interior Furnishings

Although the focal point of a church is the altar, a church's interior has other furnishings that promote devotion and piety. The character and beauty of the interior and its furnishings are to portray the holiness of the sacred mysteries. Throughout the ages, the Church has welcomed the artistic expression of every culture and has adapted to local traditions in choice of design and art. Although each church has its own unique decor, the following are ordinarily found in a Catholic church.

Holy-water font: At the entrance to a Catholic church are small receptacles that contain holy water. When Catholics enter the church, they dip their fingertips into the bowl and make the Sign of the Cross as a reminder of their commitment to Christ at baptism.

Poor box: From early times, it was customary to share one's material goods with the needy. In accordance with this tradition, a special receptacle for donations for the poor is usually near the entrance.

Statues: Since Vatican II, the liturgy is the primary faith expression for Catholics; devotion to the saints is secondary. Therefore, if there are any statues in a church, they are placed in less prominent places so as not to detract from the liturgy.

Stations of the Cross: The fourteen Stations of the Cross portray scenes of the passion and death of Christ. These plaques, statues, crosses, or symbols are hung along the walls of a Catholic church and assist Catholics in prayerfully tracing the steps of Christ's passion. The Stations of the Cross can be prayed privately or with a group and are especially meaningful to Catholics during Lent.

Sanctuary Furnishings

Since the sanctuary is the focal point of a church, the sanctuary furnishings are chosen with great care. These furnishings portray unity and harmony in design; they are liturgically correct and blend with the overall decor.

Altar: The focal point of the sanctuary is the altar or table on which the sacrifice of the Mass is offered. Made of stone or some other durable material, the altar is covered by at least one altar cloth and is left unadorned when not in use.

Lectern: The lectern is a tall stand from which the lector proclaims the sacred Word. It is usually stationary and placed so that the person reading can be easily seen and heard.

Cross: Since the Mass re-creates the sacrifice of Calvary in an unbloody manner, a cross, whether movable or fixed, must be clearly visible during Mass.

Tabernacle: The eucharistic presence of Christ is reserved in hosts that are placed in the tabernacle. This cabinetlike receptacle, which must be immovable and locked at all times, is either on a side altar or in a separate chapel.

Sanctuary lamp: As a reminder of God's constant presence in our midst and out of respect for the eucharistic presence of Christ, a special lamp burns continuously in front of the tabernacle. It can either be a large candle or a lamp with an electric bulb.

Candles and incense: Although candles no longer serve the practical purpose of providing light, they symbolize joy and festivity. They also remind us of God's revelation throughout salvation history as fire and light. At least two candles are lit on or near the altar during Mass. The more solemn the occasion, the more candles are used.

The large paschal candle, first lit in the darkness of the Easter Vigil, is used at liturgies during the Easter season and at baptisms and funerals. The paschal candle is a vivid reminder of our faith in Christ's Resurrection.

Incense has been connected with prayer since biblical times:

"Let my prayer be incense before you" (Psalm 141:2). It symbolizes communication with God through our sense of smell and the image of smoke. It is used on solemn occasions.

Other items: The presider sits on or stands by the presider's chair when he is not at the altar. It is usually positioned directly behind the altar, slightly to the right or left, facing the assembly.

Seats for the liturgical ministers are placed so ministers can conveniently move to them throughout the liturgy.

Ordinarily, a small table is positioned somewhere in the sanctuary to hold vessels and other objects when they are not in use.

Other adornments (flowers, plants, trees, banners, hangings, tapestries, and other decorations) can enhance and promote devotion. However, ornamental additions should not be overdone or placed where they distract and interfere with the liturgy.

Liturgical Directives and Books

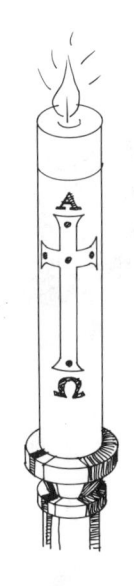

As the Mass changed from a simple, spontaneous service to formal worship, Mass prayers and readings had to be written down. Formerly, these were in Latin. Today, the books used at liturgy are in the local language and follow *The Roman Missal*. They include the diocesan and Church guidelines, books used during the liturgy, and booklets used by the assembly.

Order of Prayer: The *Order of Prayer* for the Eucharist (or *Ordo*) is a book that contains directions for each day of the liturgical year. It is published each year and specifies the local feasts and observances. An indispensable guide for the presider as he prepares for Mass, the *Order of Prayer* outlines the calendar, feasts, votive Masses, and options allowed and indicates where the readings and prayers can be found.

Sacramentary: This is a book that contains the prayers that the presiding priest uses. It is either held by the altar server when prayers are said from the chair or placed on the altar during the eucharistic prayer.

Lectionary: This book contains the Scripture readings for each day's Mass. It is carried by the lector during the entrance procession and placed on the lectern.

Commentary and general intercessions: The Mass theme and general intercessions are contained in the commentary. This is usually put at the place from which the commentator reads.

Hymnals and missalettes: These books contain the songs, Mass prayers, and responses for the day's celebration. They help the assembly participate fully in the liturgy. These books are available at the church entrances or in the pews.

Chapter 6

THE PRIMARY LITURGICAL SYMBOLS

Strictly speaking, everything in God's creation is sacred. During the liturgy, however, the raw materials of bread, wine, and water are especially sacred because they are changed into Christ himself.

Bread, Wine, and Water

Bread: Bread is the "staff of life." In the Hebrew Scriptures, bread denotes freedom and salvation in the form of manna in the wilderness and the unleavened bread eaten at Passover. Jesus, the new Passover, comes to us as bread broken and shared.

The unleavened bread we use at Mass is ordinarily in the form of thin wafers called hosts. These are made by baking a batter of flour and water on a special waffle-iron type appliance that imprints a liturgical symbol on the hosts. Hosts are often made by contemplative nuns, for whom host-making serves as a means of support.

The host that the priest uses at Mass is larger than the other hosts. It is about three inches in diameter so it can be seen when elevated at the consecration. The hosts of the people are about the size of quarters. They can be chewed or dissolved in the mouth.

Wine: From ancient times, the use of wine has been used as both a drink and a symbol of celebration. When Jesus wished to give us his precious blood, it was natural that he did so with wine.

Water: Water is the primordial element, the source of physical and spiritual life. Water was used at the Last Supper, and blood and water issued from the side of Christ on the cross. At Mass, a drop of water is mixed with the wine to symbolize the joining of divinity with humanity in our liturgy.

Sacred Vessels, Linens, and Other Items

So very sacred are the articles that come into immediate contact with the body and blood of Christ. The vessels ordinarily are consecrated by a bishop or blessed by a priest to show that they are set apart for sacred use. Sacred linens used during liturgy need to be kept scrupulously clean and handled with reverence.

Chalice and paten: The chalice is the cup that holds the wine during Mass. Made of durable material, the chalice comes in a variety of styles and shapes. The large host that the priest uses at Mass rests on a small flat dish called the paten.

Ciborium: The hosts that the faithful receive are placed in the ciborium, a wide cup with a lid. The consecrated hosts are reserved in the tabernacle in the ciborium. A pocketwatch-sized receptacle called a pyx is used by priests, deacons, or eucharistic ministers to carry the consecrated hosts to the sick.

Sacred linens: The *corporal*, a square linen cloth, is set in the center of the altar at the time of the offertory.

The sacred body and blood of Christ rest on that cloth during Mass.

The *pall*, a stiff square piece of linen, is placed on the chalice after it is filled. It protects the chalice contents.

The *purificator* is a towellike linen used to clean the chalice and sacred vessels. Two small cruets contain the water and wine. A finger bowl and finger towel are used when the priest washes his hands.

Symbolism in Dress and Color

We ordinarily dress according to the occasion. The more important the occasion, the more we pay attention to our attire. At times, our garb serves as a distinguishing mark or characteristic.

At Mass, the priest wears special apparel called vestments. In times past, these were part of their ordinary dress. By their continued use at worship, however, these vestments have acquired sacred meaning and symbolism.

Deacons' vestments: Deacons wear the stole diagonally draped over one shoulder and a large outer garment resembling an alb.

Garb for other liturgical ministers varies. Some may wear the alb or a special robe, a symbol of their ministry. Some may wear appropriate street clothes.

Alb: The alb is a long white robe secured around the waist by a cincture and is worn by the priest and ministers. It symbolizes the purity of soul necessary to celebrate the sacred mysteries.

Stole: The stole is a long scarflike vestment draped around the neck. It is the symbol of the priestly office and is worn when the priest administers any sacrament.

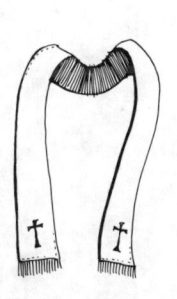

Chasuble: The chasuble is a large flowing outer garment worn specifically for liturgy. Its color reflects the liturgical season or feast, thus keeping before us the spirit of the feast.

Liturgical colors: Color is a powerful communication tool; it can produce emotional or spiritual responses.

The various liturgical colors, especially used in the presider's vestments, symbolize the deeper realities we celebrate and enable us to worship in the spirit of the season.

Red, the color of fire and blood, is worn on martyrs' feast days, Pentecost, and at confirmation celebrations.

White is a festive, joyful color. It is used during the Christmas and Easter seasons, feasts of our Lord, Mary, and saints who were not martyred. As a symbol of the Resurrection, white is also used at funerals.

Violet symbolizes repentance and penance. It is used during Advent and Lent. It can also be used at Masses for the dead.

Green is the color of anticipation and hope. It is worn during Ordinary Time, the liturgical season between Easter and Advent.

Black, symbolizing grief, is still used at funerals and Masses for the dead, although white is becoming more common.

Rose, or pink, is an optional color that can be used on special Sundays in the penitential seasons: the third Sunday of Advent and the fourth Sunday of Lent.

Although gold is not specifically a liturgical color, it adds greater solemnity to special occasions.

Body language communicates our inner emotions. Our nonverbal communication at Mass expresses our faith and shows forth our inner attitude.

Postures also symbolize a deeper reality. The postures we assume at Mass and the liturgical gestures of the presider serve in making worship more meaningful. The presider bows, genuflects, kisses the altar, extends or folds his hands. The community participates in gestures of its own.

Symbolism in Gesture and Posture

Gathering: The assembly's communal posture is the act of coming together in worship. By our gathering with other believers, we are publicly professing our faith. The uniformity of gesture and posture at Mass expresses our unity of belief.

Standing: Standing signifies respect and reverence. We stand at the beginning of Mass, during prayers, and as the gospel is read. We also stand at the end of Mass.

Sitting: There are times at Mass when we need be attentive and listen, so we sit. We sit during the readings, at the homily, and during the offering of the gifts. It's also fitting to sit after Communion.

Kneeling: Kneeling symbolizes adoration and awe in the presence of God. During Mass, we kneel at the most solemn part of the liturgy: the eucharistic prayer.

Silence: Periods of silence help us focus. We gather our personal intentions in many moments of silence: at the penitential rite when we "call to mind our sins" and after the invitation to pray, the readings, the homily, and Communion.

Chapter 7

THE LITURGICAL YEAR AND FEAST DAYS

Time seems to be an endless progression of moments, going on and on. We break the rhythm and change the pulse of time when certain spaces are seen as larger and more significant. We try to capture the full flavor of such moments by celebrating.

Our liturgical celebrations are moments in which we meld past, present, and future into a single celebration. We open up to a past reality — Christ's life and mysteries of faith — and make it present to us through liturgical worship. In the celebration of the liturgy, we enlarge Christ's life and share the fruits of Christ's Resurrection as we participate in the future promise of eternity.

Sacred Time

The Church year, with its feasts and observances, helps us appropriate the mystery of Christ into our own life. Faithfully, we relive the sacred mysteries in our own spiritual journey. We have our new beginnings, rebirths, sufferings, dyings, resurrections, and glories.

We incorporate the spirit of the Church year into our lives by being more aware of the spirit of the season and being wholly present at liturgy. Each feast and season is made special through family traditions and ethnic customs that highlight the religious significance of the feasts.

Sunday: From the time the disciples gathered to commemorate the Lord's Resurrection, Sunday has been the Christian's weekly holy day. The law for Sunday Mass was enacted in the Middle Ages as a grace and privilege because the peasants deemed themselves unworthy. In effect, the law stated, "You are equal and welcome; God knows no class distinction."

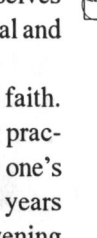

For Catholics, the Mass is a perfect act of faith. Attendance at Sunday Mass is a basic norm for practicing Catholics. Saturday evening Mass satisfies one's Sunday obligation, a carry-over from the early years of Christianity when holy days began the evening before. Since Sunday is the primary holy day, the Sunday liturgy usually has precedence over other feasts.

Holy day: A holy day is a feast that celebrates an important mystery of the Catholic faith. Catholics observe these feasts by attending Mass. The number of these holy days varies from country to country.

Catholics in the United States observe six holy days: Christmas (December 25), Solemnity of Mary, Mother of God (January 1), Ascension Thursday (forty days after Easter), Mary's Assumption (August 15), All Saints' Day (November 1), and the Immaculate Conception (December 8). In Canada, Christmas and New Year's Day are holy days; others formerly specified have either been made nonobligatory or transferred to the Sunday following.

The Liturgical Cycle

So that a greater portion and variety of Scripture is read, the liturgical year follows three cycles: A, B, and C.

Through the liturgical cycle, we relive the mysteries of faith and remember the virtues of the saints. There are two cycles within a given Church year: the Sunday, or Seasonal Cycle, and the Weekday Cycle, or Cycle of the Saints. They are also called the Proper of the Seasons and the Proper of the Saints.

The Sunday Cycle, which includes Advent, Christmas, Lent, Easter, Pentecost, and Ordinary Time recalls the life of Christ each year. Readings for the Sunday Cycle are stipulated and cannot be replaced by minor feasts. The Weekday Cycle commemorates other feasts of our Lord, Mary, and the saints.

Advent: Advent is a time of new beginnings and preparation for the coming of Christ at Christmas and in the end times. The First Sunday of Advent is the beginning of the liturgical year.

Christmastime: The two to three weeks of the Christmas season begin with Jesus' manifestation in the flesh at his birth and culminates with the celebration of the Baptism of the Lord.

Lent: Lent is the forty-day period preceding Easter; it begins on Ash Wednesday and lasts until the beginning of the Mass on Holy Thursday. Lent calls us to repentance and conversion.

Easter triduum of the Lord's passion and resurrection: The Mass on Holy Thursday evening marks the beginning of the Easter triduum. The high point of the triduum is the Easter Vigil. Only after the solemn vigil, anticipating the Resurrection, does the Easter celebration begin.

Easter: Easter Sunday commemorates the Resurrection of Jesus Christ from the dead. It holds a central place in our liturgical year.

Eastertime: The rejoicing of Easter Sunday continues throughout the Easter season: a period of fifty days, ending with the feast of Pentecost.

Pentecost: Often called "the birthday of the Church," Pentecost is celebrated fifty days after Easter. It commemorates the descent of the Holy Spirit on the apostles.

Ordinary Time: The part of the year not included in the major seasons is called Ordinary Time. It bridges the time after Christmas to Lent and from Pentecost to the First Sunday of Advent.

Weekday Cycle: The Weekday Cycle celebrates the feasts of saints, special memorials, votive Masses, and local feasts. The weekday Mass prayers and readings focus on the spirit of the feast, the saint of the day, or an optional votive Mass chosen by the presider. In the renewed liturgy, there are fewer compulsory feasts in the Proper of the Saints and more options for votive Masses and the celebration of regional or local feasts.

Mass is celebrated every day in most parishes. This custom has been in practice for several hundred years. Before that, Mass was celebrated only on Sundays and certain feasts.

Special occasions and needs: There are Mass prayers and readings for almost any time and occasion. On days when no special feast is observed, votive Masses may be offered. There are also Masses for national holidays, like July 4 and Thanksgiving Day. A special directory for children's Masses has also been compiled.

Since Mass is the most perfect prayer, Catholics often request special Masses for specific concerns or persons. The intentions or names of the persons for whom the Mass is being offered are often mentioned at the beginning of Mass as well as during the eucharistic prayer. It is customary to offer a stipend for such a Mass.

Diversity Within Unity

Although the Mass follows a basic format wherever it is celebrated around the world, we will experience a wide variety of customs and practices. We are a universal Church made up of diverse people. The style of worship is affected by the culture and ethnic customs of each country.

We get a sense of this diversity within unity when we observe the colorful liturgies the pope celebrates when he travels from country to country. I experienced this diversity myself when I was in India: the altar was low, similar to a coffee table in our culture, because people squat for worship. Candles were not available in the predominantly Hindu area, so incense sticks were used. Flowers floated in water-filled saucers, a custom in India.

Bishops can implement changes according to their cultural situations. Since each diocese within a country is made up of a variety of people, diocesan standards and norms differ.

Parishes, too, are diverse. There are sprawling suburban parishes where the people are as mobile as the seasons. There are inner-city parishes that include the homeless and destitute. There are small rural parishes made up of local farmers. There are intimate neighborhood parishes with unique ethnic customs. Each parish celebrates liturgy in a distinctive style according to the people of God who comprise it.

Within a parish, other factors affect the liturgy: the time of day, the congregation, the personality of the celebrant, the mood of the feast, the type of music, and the temperature in the building. Even within ourselves, there exists a whole gamut of liturgical diversity. If we truly believe the Mass transforms us, then each time we attend a liturgy we come as persons who have changed and grown. Although external factors affect our devotion, our inner emotions will vary from Mass to Mass. Sometimes it's hard to pray because of other "noises" in our life. There are special times, however, like weddings, baptisms, and funerals, that we cherish as never-to-be-forgotten spiritual experiences.

We should not gauge the worth of a Mass according to how "good" it makes us feel. Possibly, the times we struggle, cry out in anger to God, and feel abandoned are Masses in which God graces us most lovingly despite our emotions.

No Mass is like any other; the Mass you attend today is a once-and-for-all act of worship. We are one in the Body of Christ. Each liturgy, like each of us, is unique, special for this moment in time, for this place, by these worshipers.

Chapter 8

STRUCTURE AND PARTS OF THE MASS

Attending Mass for the first time — or for the first time after a lengthy absence — can be a wondrous and inspiring experience. To really profit and meaningfully participate, however, it helps to know what's going on. This section explains what is happening at each part of the Mass and offers suggestions for making it meaningful.

There are two main parts of the Mass: Liturgy of the Word and Liturgy of the Eucharist. The two supplementary parts, Introductory Rite and Concluding Rite, serve as "bookends" at the opening and closing of the Mass. The Liturgy of the Word focuses on the presence of Christ through the Scriptures. The Liturgy of the Eucharist focuses on the presence of Christ under the appearances of bread and wine.

Reflection Before Mass

Those gathering for Mass are about to experience a profound mystery of faith. Some quiet reflection time is necessary to fully enter into the mystery.

The following prayer serves as a suggestion for reflection before Mass:

Lord, I come to this Mass to praise and thank you. On this holy ground and in this sacred space, I remember and celebrate your presence.

No matter how solemn or simple this eucharistic liturgy will be, it is celebrated in response to your invitation, "Do this in memory of me." Thank you, Jesus, for the privilege to worship you in this way. Thank you for planting in my heart the grace to desire your presence in those gathered here today, in your sacred Word, and in the bread and wine.

I come in faith. Let it be as steady as the lit candles on the altar. May I be open to your gentle touch. May I be open to your sacred Word and listen to it as a personal challenge.

I bring to you my special needs, fears, grudges, self-pity, and petty concerns. I ask your help and guidance, Lord, to become a better person. If my cares and worries interfere with my prayer at this Mass, accept them as my feeble gifts. Transform them by your grace.

As the bread and wine will be changed into your sacramental presence, so also change me. My whole being praises, honors, and glorifies you. I come into your presence with joy.

Amen.

Introductory Rite

Those who assemble for worship come from many backgrounds and different faith orientations. They come with various needs. The Introductory Rite sets the tone and theme of the Mass. It unifies the diverse group into one worshiping community of faith.

Entrance procession: This procession sets the tone and calls the assembly to worship. On Sundays, special feasts, or special occasions, the priest and liturgical ministers enter from the rear of the church and process to the sanctuary. At times, the entire assembly will join in the procession. A suitable hymn is usually sung or an entrance psalm is recited.

Use this time to enter into the spirit of the liturgy. Put aside your concerns and be completely present to the Lord for this moment. Let it be a sacred time for you as you join in prayer and song with other believers.

Sign of the Cross: With the Sign of the Cross, we recall our baptism. The Sign of the Cross is a simple gesture we use to profess our basic belief in a trinitarian God: God the Father, our creator; God the Son, Jesus our redeemer; God the Holy Spirit, our sanctifier. It is, therefore, fitting to begin the Mass with the Sign of the Cross.

Make the Sign of the Cross with full awareness, not in a rote and haphazard manner as if shooing away flies. Profess your faith and renew your commitment to the Lord. The Sign of the Cross is a blessing for all things. Ask the Lord to bless you and all those assembled together with you.

Greeting: The priest greets the assembly with an ancient salute from our Christian tradition: "The grace and peace of God our Father and the Lord Jesus Christ be with you." Saint Paul used this same kind of spiritual greeting at the opening of his letters to the new churches. This greeting, a statement of faith, is recited five times during the Mass.

Respond "And also with you" in an audible and heartfelt manner. Gratefully reflect on the fact that you celebrate this sacred rite along with the priest and the gathered assembly.

Penitential rite: We do not come to our liturgical sacrifice as perfect persons. The penitential rite invites us to pause, recall our shortcomings, and ask God's forgiveness.

There are several ways to express our plea for mercy and forgiveness. An act of contrition recited by all ("I confess to almighty God, and to you, my brothers and sisters...") or responses to the priest's invocations ("Lord, have mercy; Christ, have mercy; Lord, have mercy") are options frequently used.

We all have our share of struggles, hurts, and clashes. We have hurt others, and we have been hurt by others. Get in touch with these conflicts, acknowledge them, and strive to be tender as was the forgiving Christ. The Eucharist brings us healing and forgiveness.

Glory to God: We come to Mass to acknowledge the greatness and goodness of God. The Glory to God, intoned by the presider, is usually sung or recited by the assembly or the choir. It's a hymn of praise similar to the praise sung by the angels at the birth of Christ.

Let your being give praise to God for the goodness that surrounds you. Think of specific graces and gifts for which you are thankful and center yourself in an attitude of gratitude.

Opening prayer: We have been forgiven and we have given praise and thanks to God. We now offer a prayer that sets the tone of the Mass. This prayer commemorates the special feast, saint of the day, or the spirit of the season. It varies with each Mass and marks the conclusion of the Introductory Rite.

As the priest recites the opening prayer, be attentive to the words. Pray along in spirit and ask for

God's grace. Respond "Amen" at the end of the prayer. During the liturgy, we will respond "Amen" eleven times. A Hebrew word which means "so be it," the "Amen" affirms what the priest prays.

Up to this point, we are a diverse group of worshipers. Although we are many, we are now one in worship of God the almighty, maker of heaven and earth.

Liturgy of the Word

Words are our basic communication tool. When we speak words with someone, we offer an intimate part of our being; we share our inner life.

God utilizes the medium of the human word as one way to remain present with us always. Although the Scriptures recount God's workings with the Jews and early Christians, they are examples of how God relates to each of us today.

God is fully present in the Liturgy of the Word. The Word becomes flesh as the Scriptures are proclaimed in the worshiping community.

Scripture readings: On Sundays and feast days, the lector reads two scriptural passages. The first reading is from the Hebrew Bible (the Old Testament) and is followed by the responsorial psalm. The second reading is a New Testament passage from the Acts of the Apostles, epistles, or the Book of Revelation. On weekdays, there is ordinarily only one reading.

Make it a point to listen to the readings — really listen. Apply the words to yourself. If one phrase leaps out, savor it. The Lord is speaking to you personally.

Responsorial psalm: We respond to the first reading with a psalm that fits the theme of the liturgy. The cantor or lector recites or chants the verses, while the assembly offers the response.

The Psalms, one hundred and fifty basic Hebrew prayers, consider every need and emotion. No matter what your prayer or need, there is a suitable psalm.

Respond to the psalm with your heart. Think of what the words mean and join with others who need the support of your prayers. Although the response might not be applicable to you, pray it for those who need it. We come to worship to build up the Body of Christ and one another.

Alleluia: Although the liturgy is in our own language, there are some words retained in their original language. *Alleluia,* the Hebrew word for "praise to you, Lord," is an acclamation before the gospel is read. It is sung or read before and after the Scripture verse that precedes the gospel.

Sing the Alleluia for what it's meant to be: an acclamation of Christ's presence in the Word of God. Sing it with gusto.

Gospel: Every liturgy includes a reading about the life of Christ as recounted in the gospels of Matthew, Mark, Luke, or John. There are a variety of readings in the renewed calendar, so over three years, most of the gospels are read.

As you use your thumb to trace a cross on your forehead and lips and over your heart, ask the Lord to be in your mind, on your lips, and in your heart so you may be worthy to be Christ for others. As the event in Jesus' life is retold, Jesus is speaking and acting in your life. He heals you, feeds you, comforts you, raises you from the dead. Allow the gospel to be a personal message addressed to you.

Homily: Homily is a comparatively new word in our Catholic vocabulary. It replaces the word *sermon*. The word *homily* comes from the Greek root that means "conversation with the people." The homily puts flesh on the Scriptures and makes practical applications to daily Christian living. It brings the Scripture readings into our own situation. Delivered by the presider or the deacon after the gospel, the homily is preached so that the community of believers may be effective Christian witnesses of the Word in the world.

Although the effectiveness of the homily is contingent on the style and manner of the preacher, the homily is not a "gauge" with which to measure the value of the liturgy. The homily not only nourishes our faith life but also challenges us to a better quality of life.

During the homily, ask yourself, *What is the Lord saying to me at this time? How can I become a better person by heeding the message I hear?* God can become present in some way if you listen creatively to the homily. Do you say to yourself as you listen to the homily, *If only so-and-so would hear this*? Why is it so easy to find something in the homily that suits someone else?

Creed: A creed is a profession of faith. The Nicene Creed expresses our basic Christian beliefs. It was formulated at the Council of Nicea in A.D. 325 and has been used since ancient times in the baptismal rite. We profess and renew our faith and baptismal commitment when we recite the Nicene Creed in our Sunday and feast-day liturgies.

The Creed is long. Follow the words in the hymn book or missalette. Recite the Nicene Creed with conviction; let it be a personal renewal of your faith and baptismal commitment. During quiet meditation time, reflect on each article of the Creed, line by line.

General intercessions: We are creatures dependent on the goodness of God. During the liturgy, we open our hearts and pray for God's help for ourselves and others. Rapid communication techniques enable us to be aware of concerns all over the world. At Mass, we join the world in praising God and offering our prayers for the needs of all people. Our intercessions are the community at worship commending the needs of the whole world to the Lord's mercy and care.

As you join in spirit with the intentions and responses, enlarge your horizons in prayerful concern for others. There will always be those with greater and lesser needs than yours. It's a time for you to exercise empathy and compassion. In the silence of your heart, bring your personal intentions and concerns before the Lord during this time.

Liturgy of the Eucharist

The Liturgy of the Eucharist recalls the words and actions of Jesus at the Last Supper. Jesus took bread and wine and offered thanks to God. He then blessed and broke the bread and gave it to those at table with him. "Do this in memory of me" (Luke 22:19). Thus, Jesus established a special way to remain with us throughout all time.

In the early years of the Church, this ritual was simple and part of the meal. As the Church spread, the liturgy became more structured. In our liturgy today, we retain the basic pattern of the Lord's Supper with additional rituals and prayers.

Presentation of gifts and collection: Before the bread and wine become the body and blood of Christ, the worshiping community presents them as gifts. Members of the assembly take these gifts in procession to the altar.

When the early Christians gathered to worship, they brought food and material goods to be shared with the less fortunate. Today, we likewise share and support our church through the collection. In many parishes, the collection basket is presented at the altar with the bread and wine.

As the gifts are brought up, ask yourself what gifts you have to offer the Lord at this time. Be generous in your support of the church. Offer your talents, work, endeavors, friends, and family as well as your cares and concerns. As the bread and wine will be transformed, so also we ask the Lord to transform us.

Prayer over the gifts: The priest offers to God the bread and the wine into which he has mixed some water. This action signifies humanity's sharing in divinity as well as divinity sharing in humanity.

In biblical times, the Jewish response to God's blessings was the *berakoth*. This Jewish blessing, basically an exclamation of praise, blessed God for some blessing, some good thing. It was used both formally and informally, any time the Jews praised God.

The priest prays this blessing as he offers the bread and wine to God: "Blessed are you, Lord, God of all creation...."

Join in with a hymn sung during this part of the Mass. If there is no hymn, respond to the blessings with "Blessed be God for ever."

The priest then washes his hands as a symbol of purification and invites us to pray that our offering may be worthy and acceptable before the Lord. A short prayer recalls the theme or feast and prepares us for the solemn eucharistic prayer.

As you respond to the invitation that your sacrifice be acceptable, include in your heart a plea for purification and worthiness to come before the Lord. Your "Amen" to the prayer concludes the offering of gifts.

Beginning of the eucharistic prayer: In dialogue form, the priest beckons us to lift our hearts to the Lord and to give thanks and praise to God. We recall how great and wonderful are God's saving events through the ancient people and through Jesus' coming to earth. This prayer, called the Preface, varies with the seasons and feasts. In unified song or prayer, we acclaim the holiness of God in the words of the prophet Isaiah: "Holy, holy, holy..." (Isaiah 6:3).

Let your soul be open to the awe and majesty of God. As creatures, we bow before the Lord in thanks and praise. We prepare for the great gift of Jesus himself in the bread and wine. Let your spirit be caught up in the mystery of Love.

Eucharistic narrative and consecration: Each liturgy recounts what Jesus said and did at the Last Supper. The priest reenacts that solemn scene and brings Christ again into our midst through the words of consecration: "This is my body....This is the cup of my blood." This is the most solemn part of the Mass. The host and chalice are raised for silent adoration and prayer.

In reverent awe and praise, become aware of Jesus now present on the altar. The bread and wine have been transformed into a sacred reality; pray that the Lord may transform us to be his presence in the world.

Acclamation of faith: After Jesus becomes eucharistically present, the priest invites the assembly to join in acclaiming this sacred mystery. The response varies and is recited or sung as a public affirmation of faith.

Let your acclamation be a hearty "Welcome, Lord." Christ's presence is renewed in a unique way: Christ is present to us in this church at this time as never before.

Eucharistic prayer continued: We believe that through Christ's death and resurrection we are united with the entire communion of saints. In the eucharistic prayer, we remember the saints and angels, our beloved dead, the Church throughout the world, and our community gathered in worship. The priest prays that through the holy sacrifice, which has made our peace with God, peace may come into the world. We pray that the salvation by Christ be brought to fulfillment. Although there are several eucharistic prayers the priest can use, each one expresses the same sentiments.

At the close of the eucharistic prayer, the priest elevates the host and the chalice. The priest offers the body and blood of Christ to God in threefold praise: "Through him, with him, in him...."

Unite yourself with the priest during the eucharistic prayer. At the end, respond with an energetic "Amen." Because this "Amen" is most solemn, it may be sung several times.

Lord's Prayer: The Lord's Prayer is fittingly placed after the eucharistic prayer as a preparation for Communion. Given us by Jesus himself, the Our Father is a powerful sign of our unity with Christ and with one another. It contains the basic elements of a true Christian prayer: we praise and thank God, we forgive one another, and we pray for needs in this life and the world to come.

"Say the Lord's Prayer, but take an hour to do it," recommended Saint Teresa of Avila. Do this in your private prayer time; savor the wealth contained in this perfect prayer. You will then appreciate it more fully when you join in saying the Lord's Prayer with others at Eucharist.

Doxology after the Lord's Prayer: The early Christians drew many rituals from their Jewish heritage. One such ritual was a triple praise called a "doxology," used to end their prayers. At the end of the Lord's Prayer, the priest asks the Lord to deliver us from every evil and to grant us peace and protection as we wait for the Lord's coming. The assembly responds, "For the kingdom, the power, and the glory are yours now and for ever." Protestants have traditionally used a form of this doxology at the end of the Lord's Prayer. Its use in the Mass is the revival of an ancient Christian custom.

Sign of peace: From earliest times, Christians exchanged the kiss of peace as a way to show they were all one Body in Christ. The sign of peace we share before Communion expresses our reconciliation with one another. With a nod, handshake, kiss, or embrace, we recall Jesus' words, "...if you bring your gift to the altar, and there recall that your brother has anything against you, leave your gift there at the altar, go first and be reconciled with your brother, and then come and offer your gift" (Matthew 5:23-24).

In peace and love, extend yourself to those near you. Although you might not know the person next to you, the two of you are united through Christ. The peace we offer is the peace of Christ; include in your heart all those you need to forgive.

Breaking of the bread and the "Lamb of God": The early Christians called their gathering the "breaking of the bread." The priest breaks the large host as a sign that we are one by sharing in the one bread.

While the priest prepares the hosts for distribution at Communion, the assembly recites the invocation that John the Baptist uttered when he saw Jesus: "Behold, the Lamb of God, who takes away the sin of the world" (John 1:29). The image of the lamb represents Jesus as the new Passover; through the shedding of his blood, he has saved us. The invocation is recited three times. The first two times, we ask for mercy; the last time, we ask the Lord to grant us peace.

Recite the Lamb of God with full conviction that your sins are forgiven through Jesus. Then you can mirror Christ joyfully to others.

Communion preparation: Before we receive Christ in the bread and wine, the priest invites the assembly to join in a common preparation prayer. The priest reverently raises the wine and host and announces, "This is the Lamb of God who takes away the sins of the world. Happy are those who are called to his supper."

Respond humbly and with deep conviction of the mercy of God. We pray with the same words the centurion in the gospel used when he asked Jesus to heal his son: "Lord, I am not worthy to receive you, but only say the word and I shall be healed."

Reception of holy Communion: It's remarkable that God has become man. It's more wonderful to consider that he died a most atrocious death for us. But it's a mind-boggling mystery of faith when we realize that Jesus continues his presence with us through common ordinary food and drink: bread and wine. This belief is one of the most sacred mysteries of our faith.

It is proper and more complete to receive Communion when we attend Mass. The Eucharist is an experience of healing and forgiveness. However, Catholics still follow the practice of going to confession before Communion if they have severed their relationship with the Lord through serious sin.

Eucharistic ministers and deacons assist in distributing Communion as needed.

The Eucharist is normally received during liturgy. We are encouraged to receive Communion each time we attend Mass.

Traditionally, one fasts from food and drink — except for water and medicine — for at least one hour before receiving Communion.

You may choose to receive Communion on the tongue or in your hand. When the host is offered to you, respond "Amen." Let this response be a conscious act of faith. Your "Amen" says, "Yes, Lord, I really believe that receiving you in a consecrated piece of bread changes me. May I mirror your goodness through your coming into my being and becoming part of me."

Receiving the body and blood of Christ in the host is the ordinary manner of reception. Christ is totally present under each form, however. When Communion is offered in the host and also as wine from the cup, you can opt to receive Communion under both forms. The cup containing the body and blood of

Christ as wine can be offered regularly, if practical, and on special occasions.

Concluding Rite

Thanksgiving after Communion: A hymn might be sung while Communion is being distributed. A period of quiet after one receives Communion provides time for personal prayer.

The time after Communion is a sacred time; the Lord is closely united with us. Use this time to recommit yourself to the Lord and present your deepest concerns in prayer.

Communion prayer: As the Eucharist draws to an end, we join in a common, final prayer, the post-Communion prayer, before we receive the final blessing.

As you respond "Amen," gather in spirit all the prayers of those united with you at this worship.

The liturgy is drawing to a close. Renewed in the Word of God and the body and blood of Christ, the community begins to orient itself toward carrying Christ into the world. From the intensity of prayer and praise, Catholics return to the reality of daily routines.

Announcements: Since the Sunday liturgy is the only time the whole community is gathered together, announcements are appropriate at this time. Information about parish programs and events, letters from the bishop, or other relevant items of interest are brought to the community's attention. Anyone may address the assembly at this time.

As you hear of activities and other opportunities for greater involvement, ask yourself how you can become more active in your parish. Become an involved Catholic; share your talents and time.

Blessing: If a deacon is present, he announces, "Bow your heads and pray for God's blessing." Though various words and forms may be used, the blessing is given by the priest, who makes the Sign of the Cross over the assembly.

Gather all personal and community intentions into one as you bow your head. As you make the Sign of the Cross, respond "Amen," asking the Lord to give you strength and wisdom to respond to the power of grace working through you.

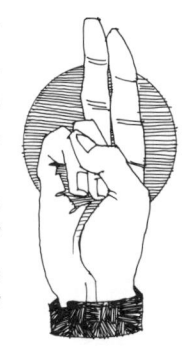

Commissioning to go forth: After the priest blesses the assembly, a deacon, if present, dismisses the assembly with the challenge: "The Mass is ended; go in peace…to love and serve the Lord." The celebration of the Mass is over, but its fruits of goodness must be carried into the marketplace.

Your response, "Thanks be to God," is a "Yes, Lord, I am determined to leave this Mass energized, with the grace of God, to continue to be Christ's presence in the world."

Recessional: While the liturgical ministers leave the church in procession, an instrumental postlude is played or a recessional hymn is sung by the assembly or choir. It's common courtesy to remain in place until the priest and ministers leave.

Reflection After Mass

Leaving church with the right orientation is just as important as beginning Mass with the right orientation. To rush from the pew without taking the time to quietly reflect on the profound mystery of faith that has just been celebrated is a discredit to the Body of Christ.

The following prayer serves as a suggestion for reflection after Mass:

The candles have been extinguished and the altar is clear. But the Mass continues. We who have worshiped together will now scatter the fruits of this Mass as we go our separate ways. As I leave, Lord, I reflect on your challenge to "go into the world to make disciples of all nations."

I have been favored and strengthened with your sacramental presence. With this renewed strength and spiritual energy, I can face all the challenges of life and "be eucharist" to all those I meet along life's way.

In the days ahead, may I realize what's really important in life and order my behavior accordingly. When I am impatient, may I be calmed by your patient love. When I am frustrated, may I be consoled by your peace.

Let me heal the wounds of our fractured world and bring about wholeness and hope. Let me be the leaven through which wholesome goodness and holiness rise in our world. May I carry your love to the unloved.

With great awe and deep gratitude, I take you with me as the Bread of Life. It is a profound privilege to be your hands, your ears, your feet, and your heart for others.

Amen.

The Mass Continues

Sunday liturgy is an opportunity for parish togetherness. Some parishes provide a hospitality time after the Sunday liturgy. People linger to share family, parish, and community concerns.

Make use of this opportunity to get to know other

parishioners and to put the fruits of the Mass into practice.

Although our celebration is over, the Mass continues to vibrate as we go on our individual ways. Our actions and presence in the world can mirror Christ. Leave with a determination that you will reflect Christ to all you meet in your home, the workplace, and in the world.

CONCLUSION

"There are also many other things that Jesus did, but if these were to be described individually, I do not think the whole world would contain the books that would be written" (John 21:25). The same can be said about the Mass. Tomes could be written about its rich history, elegant theology, and profound mystery.

I hope this booklet provides adequate information and material for prayerful reflection. May these words support you in your spiritual journey; they certainly have supported me. I have become sensitive to the many nuances involved in liturgy and the rich spiritual treasures it offers. The most profound insights were not gleaned from the theological treatises and liturgical directives I researched. Rather, quiet moments of reflection and conscious participation in Mass led me into renewed intimacy with our Lord.

Our faith is like our expansive universe. The more we probe, the more we find: the more we find, the deeper spiritual riches are ours; the more the spiritual truths are revealed, the more we are caught up in the wonder, mystery, and love of God.

I make the words of Saint Augustine my own: "To search for God is a challenging human adventure; to find God is the noblest human achievement; to fall in love with God is life's highest fulfillment."

May you find a key here that opens for you the rich spiritual growth that the experience of the liturgy can be.